ADI'S PERFECT PATTERNS AND LOOPS

written by Caroline Karanja

illustrated by Ben Whitehouse

raintree
a Capstone company — publishers for children

Meet our creative coders!

This is Adi. Adi likes arts and crafts. She spends most of her time colouring, playing music and making things. Whenever she sees something new, she wonders how it came to be. She likes to say, "I wonder . . ."

This is Gabi. Gabi loves to read, play outside and take care of her dog, Charlie. She is always curious about how things work. Whenever she sees something that needs fixing, she tries to find the best way to improve it. She often says, "What if . . .?"

Adi and Gabi make a great team!

Gabi is going to Adi's house after school today. When the bus gets to their stop, the girls thank the driver and get off. He waves and drives to his next stop.

Gabi's dog, Charlie, comes to meet them. "Hello, Charlie!" the girls say.

The post woman arrives in her van. She is delivering post to the houses nearby. "Hello, Ms Cruz!" the girls call out.

"Hello, girls!" Ms Cruz says.

"Do you have lots of stops today?" Gabi asks.

"The same stops every day!" Ms Cruz replies.

"Just like the bus driver!" Adi says.

POST WOMAN'S LOOP

PICK UP POST

⬇

DELIVER POST

⬇

MOVE TO NEXT HOUSE

"Yep! The bus driver and I make our loops every day – pick up, deliver, repeat!" Ms Cruz says, then hops back in her van and drives down the road.

BUS DRIVER'S LOOP

DROP / PICK UP PASSENGERS

↓

DRIVE TO NEXT STOP

"Do you know who else makes loops?" Gabi says to Adi. "Computer programmers! They make loops so that they don't have to repeat commands."

"Instead of giving the same instructions every time a task has to be repeated, programmers make a code loop that repeats the instructions for them. Then the computer will follow the repeating pattern until the job is finished," Gabi says.

"A bus driver and a post woman use loops to perform the same tasks at every stop they make!" Adi adds. "I wonder what other jobs have loops?"

"Lots!" Gabi says. "In factories, restaurants or offices, lots of jobs run on loops. The same tasks are repeated again and again until the job is finished."

What is a loop?

In a computer, a loop is a block of code that tells the computer to repeat a task until it's completed. Programmers can add statements such as if/then statements in their code loop. For example: If there is someone at the bus stop, then the driver will stop. If there is no one waiting, then the driver will keep going.

Inside the house, Adi sees a large box near the front door. Adi's mum says, "Look what the post woman has delivered! Grandpa sent it."

Adi opens it and finds a train set. "Wow!" she says. "Do you want to help me build the track, Gabi?"

"Yes!" Gabi agrees.

The girls take the box to the living room. The train set has pieces of track and different types of train carriages. It also has some buildings, a remote control and even some small people.

The girls work on building their track. It has straight parts, curved parts and bridges.

"Our train has a route, like the bus driver and the post woman. It also has to repeat tasks at every station," Adi says.

"What if we give the train a code loop to help it do its tasks?" Gabi suggests.

"Great idea! We can make train stations with these," Adi says, holding up one of the buildings. "At each station, the train can run its code loop."

Using loops in code

All kinds of computer games and applications use loops. A website for online shopping might have a loop that tells it to send a thank you email to the customer every time a purchase is made. In a computer game, you might see a dancing character who does the same action again and again. It's because a programmer has put it on a loop!

"Now let's make the train," Gabi says.

"Our train is like the block of code," Adi says. "We have to build the code so that it knows what to do at each stop."

"Right!" Gabi agrees. "Our train has three tasks: move to a station, drop things off and pick things up."

"Things and people!" Adi says.

15

"OK, let's build our code blocks. First the engine. Its task is to stop the train at each station." Gabi makes a small sign that says *MOVE TO NEXT STATION* and tapes it to the engine.

MOVE TO NEXT STATION
↓
DROP OFF PEOPLE AND PACKAGES
↓
PICK UP PEOPLE AND PACKAGES

Adi decides that the blue carriage's task will be to drop off packages and people that belong at each station. She makes a sign that says *DROP OFF*, and she tapes it to the blue carriage.

The red carriage's task will be to pick up packages or people from each station. The girls tape a sign to the red carriage that says *PICK UP*.

DROP OFF

PICK UP

MOVE TO NEXT STATION

"We've built our code. Shall we see if it works?" Adi asks.

"Of course! You can be the computer programmer – like the engineer!" Gabi says. She hands Adi the remote control.

"All aboard!" Adi calls out and starts the train.

"*Choo choo!*" the girls say as the train rounds the bend. When it gets to the first station, Adi stops the train. Gabi takes a toy block off the train and leaves it at the station. She puts two people waiting at the station on to the train.

"Our code works!" Adi cheers.

Gabi says, "Let's run the loop again! *Chugga chugga choo choo!*"

Can you make a code loop?

Adi and Gabi will be selling home-made cookies in their local area. Using a toy or your finger, trace the route they should take to each house. They will have four repeating tasks. What order should the tasks go in? Can you write a code loop for them?

Tasks

GIVE THEM COOKIES

RING DOORBELL

ASK IF THEY WANT COOKIES

TAKE PAYMENT

Glossary

code one or more rules or commands to be carried out by a computer

command instruction that tells a computer to do something; many commands put together make up computer programs

loop something that happens again and again

pattern repeated sequence; things that follow in a specific order

programmer person who writes code that can be run by a machine

task piece of work that needs to be done

Think in code!

- What tasks do you do every morning or evening? How does your daily loop start? How does it end?

- Patterns are everywhere. Create a pattern that alternates between different numbers. Try a pattern that alternates between different shapes and colours.

- Write a code loop to use every time you make your favourite sandwich. In what order should the ingredients go in the sandwich? Tape the code loop inside your cupboard for a reminder the next time you make lunch!

About the author

Caroline Karanja is a developer and designer who is on a mission to increase accessibility and sustainability through technology. She enjoys discovering how things work and sharing this knowledge with others. She lives in Minnesota, USA.

Raintree is an imprint of Capstone Global Library Limited, a company incorporated in England and Wales having its registered office at 264 Banbury Road, Oxford, OX2 7DY – Registered company number: 6695582

www.raintree.co.uk
myorders@raintree.co.uk

Edited by Kristen Mohn
Designed by Kay Fraser
Design Element: Shutterstock/Arcady
Original illustrations © Capstone Global Library Limited 2019
Originated by Capstone Global Library Ltd
Printed and bound in India

ISBN 978 1 4747 5921 2
22 21 20 19 18
10 9 8 7 6 5 4 3 2 1

British Library Cataloguing in Publication Data
A full catalogue record for this book is available from the British Library.